Songs, Praise and Joy

Songs, Praise and Joy

JOHN ALEXANDER

DEDICATION

Dedicated to those who love songs, praise and joy.

CONTENTS

ACKNOWLEDGEMENTS

I wish to acknowledge my wife for her patience and encouragement as I write and for her seeds of inspiration to get me started.

I want to thank the Mockingbird chapter of the Poetry Society of Texas for the feedback and encouragement to continue writing.

I want to acknowledge Craig and Karen Ruhl at Faith On Every Corner magazine who allow me to share my poems around the globe as part of their monthly magazine.

A special offer of thanks and gratitude goes out to friends in the Marathon Class and the Men's Bible study group for their interest and encouragement as I continue to write.

A thank you goes out to friends and followers on QuietTimeRhymes.com and Facebook who are a constant stream of encouragement as they read my words, offer comments, and share their support.

SONG OF THE SOUL

Inside this old body that's older each year
Lives a soul that's eternal, so what should I fear?
If I dwell on the temporal things that don't last,
I will miss the important; regret the days past.

This journey on earth that I measure by time,
Is a song to be written, with rhythm and rhyme.
The verses I write as I go through each day
Are penned by my acts, what I feel, think, or say.

God help me take time to show others respect;
Reach out, lend a hand; display love not neglect;
Form bonds and relationships, ties that are strong;
Make people feel valued and know they belong.

Help me focus on others in word and in deed;
May my words shine a light that can touch a soul's need.

YOUR SONG

You write each line, each verse, my life.
Some fill with gladness others strife.
I pray Your stanzas form my song
Each word and note where they belong.

I pray my life reflects Your word,
May You be seen; Your song be heard.
Lord write Your song upon my heart
Grant me today a brand-new start.

Lord write your verse through word and deed
Keep me attuned to others' need.
Lord keep my eyes on You today.
Lord light my path show me the way

To live my life that it may rhyme
And play each note in perfect time.
Lord touch my life, adjust each string,
Give me the words Your song to sing.

A NEW SONG

We write what's inside, it comes out in our life
Regardless of heartaches from troubles and strife.
We all have a song that we sing with our soul.
The verses we learn as the years take a toll.

I pray that the lines you recite in your head,
Bring hope to the children with wisdom you spread,
In this world full of turmoil, confusion and hate,
I pray for new voices before it's too late.

May history give us the insight we need
To not spiral downward in word and in deed.
I pray for a change, for a breath of fresh air.
May the children find hope and not sink in despair.

May the next generation discern wrong from right,
Rebel against darkness, be drawn to the light.
Instill a new song in our youth that brings joy.
May Your love fill the heart of each girl and each boy.

HEART SONGS

If I dug deep for words to say,
What kind of song would my heart play?
If I could write what I hold dear,
Would others read, and would they hear?

If I could find the words to share,
Would others hear and would they care?
Would words express the way I feel?
Could words I share help others heal?

Could words touch chords, strum strings inside,
Reach deep within where hope resides?
If words I weave turned into song,
Would there be those who sing along?

Could music grow from just one note
And birth a song from words I wrote?
I'll share my heart and write each word.
I'll sing my song, know God has heard.

IF MY SOUL SANG

If my soul sang, what kind of song
Would it sing out the whole day long?
What kind of rhythm would emerge,
A joyful beat, or mournful dirge?

What kind of melody would form
To offer comfort, calm the storm?
Would I sing slow, a soothing tone,
That's just for me when I'm alone?

Or would I sing out loud and share
A song of comfort, love, and care?
What makes a song, just tune and word,
Or what is felt when it is heard?

A song can bring a change in mood,
I pray my soul serves healthy food.
I pray the words of rhyme I write
Help other souls to soar in flight.

I pray the lyrics I prepare
Come from the heart, God's love to share.

HEART SONG

For You oh Lord I share my song.
I give You praise the whole day long.
I know Your love and my heart sings
The joy inside Your Spirit brings.

You gave me life. You set me free,
Unlocked the door, Lord You're the key.
When days grow dark You are my light.
Your Holy Spirit gives me sight.

I pray my eyes are fixed on You.
Help me discern what's pure and true.
I pray that I reflect Your Word
If this, my song, is one day heard.

I pray Your words from my heart flow,
Help others hear and come to know
The love that I have found in You,
And know Your joy in their heart too.

LIVE OUR SONG

Lord help me reach inside of me
To find the songs and set them free.
So many songs inside my heart,
Each one unique and set apart.

I pray the words that I write down
Reflect the joy and peace I've found.
I pray my songs help others find
The person, Lord, that You designed.

Uniquely formed from all the rest,
Lord set them free to be their best.
We've each been blessed with gifts and song
For us to sing our whole life long.

Help me to live my song today.
Lord tune my heart and words I say.
I'm no one else, I'm only me.
I thank you Lord I've been set free.

SOUL SONG

Lord knows I'm gettin' weary and my walk's a little slow.
My hair has turned to silver, but my heart still has a glow.
My mind is still a dancin', but the spring has left my step.
I can't remember when it was that through the night I slept.

My head's still overflowing with the things I'd like to do,
But my body sings a different tune, "Let's only pick a few."
If I try to overdo it, then my bones respond with hurt.
My body wants me sitting down, my mind is still alert.

The body's weak and slowing down,
      the mind's still going strong.
The two don't mix, we coexist, but we don't get along.
Perhaps a soul bound up inside a body weak and frail,
Begins to learn new ways to cope,
      to spread its wings and sail.

I read, I pray, and listen, then I wait until I've heard.
I seek the truth, then write it down,
      I try to spread the word.
Someday I'll leave this frame behind,
      transcend this earthly plane,
And rise to heights I've never seen, can never here attain.

A COUNTRY SONG

If I could write a country song
I'd pen a tune that's smooth and long
Share what I know, not hesitate,
That true love's real and worth the wait

I'd write of love that's strong and true
I'd play a melody for you
Of love that's grown through many years
A love that lasts through joy and tears

Just watch the birds glide through the sky
See beauty in a butterfly
Allow your heart to sing along
You'll find true love it won't be long

Just take it slow don't go too fast
It takes some work to make it last
In love commitment is the key
For love to flourish, healthy, free

I'd play that song around the world
To every boy and every girl
Let others know the way I feel
I'd share with them that love is real

THE SONG

As I come before God, and I lift up my prayer,
I am joining with the others as part of a song.
My words a small part, yet He's fully aware
Of each word of the prayer that is centuries long.

Each day we His people lift prayers to the Lord
As we join in the stream of words ancient and old,
Conversations with God whom we love and adore,
A message unbroken that never grows cold.

I consider the saints who are part of that stream,
The prayers they have lifted in days long ago.
I give thanks for each one that the Lord has redeemed.
The number of prayers I'm sure only God knows.

The prayers that we're lifting each day from the heart
Become part of a song and we each sing a part.

LET LOVE SING

I need to write about the things I feel.
I need to share what I have learned is real.
I need to share if no one else will hear.
It doesn't matter if there's no one near.

Sometimes I shout it from a mountain top.
Sometimes I whisper but the words won't stop.
It makes me mellow when I hear it rain,
The lonesome whistle of a distant train.

I love to walk along a wooded trail,
To hear the music of a nightingale.
I love the flowers when they bloom in spring,
To watch an eagle as it spreads its wings.

I love the beauty of a well-formed song,
Each note exactly where it should belong,
Along with words that stir inside of me
A revelation that will set me free.

I pray that each of us will find a way
To show our love to others every day.
We're each an instrument and play a part,
A song of beauty when we share our heart.

SING ALONG

I'd like to pen a lively tune,
A song that anyone can croon,
A song that puts a little pep
Into our walk, our stride, our step.

I love the songs that bring a smile,
That help us laugh just for a while.
I love to see your smiling face.
Just hum along, pick up the pace.

If you can't whistle, hum, or sing,
Then grab a bell and let it ring.
Join in the chorus shout it out,
Sing loud and clear and leave no doubt.

Let's tell the world we have a song.
We're gonna sing it all day long.

FREE TO SING

I pray that soon I'll laugh once more.
I'm often much too focused now.
I ponder what life has in store
As though I'm in control somehow.

I do my best, I live each day.
I'm prone to think I'm in control
Of all the things that come my way,
But must admit that's not my role.

God holds my future in His hand.
My trust in Him can set me free.
I need not fully understand,
He'll light my path and help me see.

Embrace the joy the Lord can bring.
God's in control. We're free to sing.

MY LIPS CAN PRAISE

My lips can praise the lord my God,
                              my eyes can see his light.
His spirit guides my path through life,
                              he shows me what is right.
I praise you precious Jesus, you took me by the hand.
You carried me through waters rough and safely to dry land.

I'll praise you on the mountain, and in the valleys deep,
I know your love surrounds me it's mine to know and keep.
Lord lift my eyes toward heaven to see your shining face.
I know you're there preparing for me a dwelling place.

Through streets of gold one day we'll walk,
                              I'll know your perfect peace.
Your light will shine through heaven's sky
                              and earthly time will cease.
I'll meet your saints in glory and sing angelic songs.
The glory of your precious name
                              will bless the heavenly throngs.

Lord keep my soul until that day I see you face to face,
I praise your name for your great love
                              that saved me by your grace.

GIVE PRAISE

Some nights are long with little sleep,
Devoid of rest that's long and deep.
Yet life goes on, it does not wait,
It's never early, never late.

Today the sun will rise once more.
Each day's unique, not lived before.
New challenges to overcome,
I know today I'm facing some.

I pray I keep my eyes on You
To give me strength to carry through.
Help me maintain a steady pace,
Meet every challenge that I face.

Help me complete each task this day
To honor You in every way,
To lift your name and give you praise
Until the time you end my days.

ALL PRAISE

If I were a flower that blooms in the spring,
I would praise my creator to Him I would sing.
If I were a mountain I'd reach to the sky
I'd give God the glory and praise Him on high.

If I were an ocean or even a sea,
I'd praise God for the life that is teeming in me.
If I were a tree I would offer my fruits,
As a praise to the God who gives strength to my roots.

If I were a cluster of grapes on the vine,
I would offer myself to my God for fine wine.
If I were a gemstone asleep in the night,
I'd praise God every morning reflecting His light.

All God's creations know how they were made.
They know their creator the memory won't fade.
He gave us dominion o'er all of the earth.
Why don't we all praise Him who formed us at birth?

PRAISE HIM

We lift up our voices Lord praising your name.
You are worthy oh Lord to receive all our praise.
That's why we are here, it's the reason we came.
Your love is forever, not measured in days.

You came as a man made of flesh and of bone.
The angels sang praises as Mary gave birth.
There's no greater love that has ever been known.
Your power and majesty permeate earth.

Your name is the sweetest that we'll ever hear,
You are the Holy one, God's only Son,
A name angels praise and one demons all fear.
With glory and honor You fought, and You won.

We lift up our voices with angels we sing.
We offer in song all the praises we bring.

JOY

As shadows cross my soul, my mind,
I search your Word; may joy I find.
Lord shine your light into the gloom.
Drive out the shadows from the room.

May Your light burn, Lord, like a fire.
Instill in me Your heart's desire,
That I may know abundant life,
And find your joy amidst the strife.

I see Your light. The day is new.
The darkness fades. The sky is blue.
Throw open doors and windows too,
And let Your light come shining through.

Bring forth in me Your joy inside.
Fill up each nook, let nothing hide.
Let joy spring forth into a song
That I may sing the whole day long.

ENDLESS JOY

I trust in God, his master plan.
He knows the years of my life's span.
He knows how long I'll spend on earth.
I look to Him for my life's worth.

The day will come I'll be set free,
Know endless joy eternally.
I pray that when my life is done,
When Christ says welcome home my son,

That those I leave behind that day,
Whose lives I've touched in some small way,
Rejoice and lift their voice in song
And know I'm home where I belong.

I pray that you who've read this rhyme
Don't fear the day when it's your time,
That you know Christ who gives you peace,
Your life with Him will never cease.

MELODIES OF JOY

Embrace the truth that's in God's Word,
The purest songs you've ever heard.
Each word a note to form a score,
Each verse to last forevermore.

Inside God's Word are songs of old
That warm the heart when it's grown cold.
You'll hear the melodies of joy,
Those soothing words we still enjoy.

Some tunes are sad like some today.
They turned from God and lost their way.
So sweet the sound when they returned,
Embraced His love, their lesson learned.

His Word's a song inside our heart.
It only takes one note to start.
His melodies and words are there.
They've been preserved for all to share.

GROW JOY

I pray these simple words today
Will soothe your heart in some small way.
No matter what you're going through,
Or what you have in front of you,

I pray for strength to reach your goal.
I pray for peace inside your soul.
I pray new heights you can attain,
That your hard work is not in vain.

I pray you're loved by trusting friends,
On whom you always can depend.
I pray you share the life you live,
Each day you find a way to give,

To use the things you've done and know
To help another learn and grow.
As you find wisdom to impart,
I pray that joy grows in your heart.

JOYFUL SPIRIT

I bring you a sonnet; I can't end your pain.
I pray as you listen, you let your soul soar.
I pray you find love as you read each refrain.
I pray for a moment the pain you'll ignore.

I wish I could help you to know life pain free,
Remove all the ailments your body has known,
To walk in the sunshine, cause hurting to flee.
I pray your soul's joyful though your body may groan.

I pray that your body will find ways to heal
No longer restrict you and tug at your soul.
I pray you find freedom to match how you feel
To soar as an eagle, new sights to behold.

I pray that the sonnet that I pen with love,
Will help you find peace that God sends from above.

PURE JOY

My soul to heaven soon will rise,
I'll look into my Savior's eyes.
I'll find pure joy, fulfilled at last,
I'll know His love, discard the past.

No need for fear, all evil's done.
We'll celebrate. The battle's won.
I'll lift my voice, give God my praise.
New revelations will amaze,

To know pure love forevermore,
See sights I never seen before.
His majesty is all around,
Angelic chorus, what a sound.

My soul will rise and leave this place,
Beyond the bounds of time and space.

FINDING JOY

If I climbed every mountain, or learned how to fly,
Yet knew not the one who created the sky,
I'd keep looking and searching to find the next thrill,
Hoping to find it just over the hill.

There's always an ad for a new thing to try,
Offering something if only we'll buy,
Perhaps it is happiness, beauty, or fame.
In the end we find out that we're still just the same.

No human philosophy mankind provides
Can fulfill the longing for God that's inside.
Lord help me to see that I only need You.
In You I find rest, not in things that I do.

There's joy in the person of Jesus my King.
Lord You give me peace, with Your joy I can sing.

JOY AND PEACE

No matter what the year may bring
May you find joy, may your heart sing.
May you find peace in spite of storms,
God's love inside to keep you warm.

Life brings the best and worst of times.
Our roots reach deep through dirt and grime
To gain the strength we need to grow.
Look up and feel God's love and know

Our life on earth is not the end.
No matter what's around the bend
God's love's eternal, pure, and strong.
He walks with us the whole day long.

May you know joy and peace this year
Throughout the ups and downs and tears.

CHOOSE JOY

As I search for the words to describe how I feel,
And reach deep in my heart to share something that's real,
I pray I'm reflecting God's light from above,
The words that I share are expressions of love.

At times when I'm weary and troubles abound
I need time with the Lord, morning silence, no sound.
That time, early morning, to read and to pray
To help me refocus, prepare for the day,

Remember the Lord is in charge of my life.
His Spirit's inside me through troubles and strife.
Why should I choose worry, get all weighted down,
When the Lord offers joy and a smile not a frown?

You are the love that I find in my heart.
You bring joy every morning before the day starts.

FIND JOY

We're frail and we're human. We're made out of clay.
Our Father's in heaven, we're children of light.
We think we are strong, and we wander astray.
We escape under darkness, the cover of night.

Why the attraction of evil and harm?
What's so alluring that pulls us to choose
Evil not virtue? I don't see the charm.
It's a path to destruction there's so much to lose.

What good is a mountain of silver or gold,
Or a room full of trophies and plaques and awards,
If you gain the whole world and you give up your soul?
Life's full of illusions that shatter in shards.

Father is waiting in heaven above.
May our hearts fill with joy from the true source of love.

GO FORTH IN JOY
(Inspired by Isaiah 55:12)

The Lord goes before you so go out with joy.
His strength is your virtue it's yours to enjoy.
Follow the Lord and be led with His peace.
Find His joy in your heart and it never will cease.

From the mountains hear shouting, great joy they proclaim,
And also, the hills hear them echo the same,
Announcing the joy that inside you is found.
From the hills and the mountains, it's such a sweet sound.

Even the trees are not silent or still.
They join in the chorus with mountains and hills.
They clap and applaud like the beat of a drum,
Or the strings of a harp or guitar that they strum.

Go forth in joy and know peace from above.
The Lord God is with you as you spread His love.

ABOUT THE AUTHOR

I live in Frisco, Texas with my wife and our spoiled Caviler Spaniel, Lucy. I began writing rhymes in the spring of 2017. I began writing rhymes during my quiet time February 2020. Writing is my passion and I will continue to write more rhymes. I would love to hear from you. Visit my website, browse my blog, find me on Facebook and drop me a note.

Blessings,
John Alexander

QuietTimeRhymes.com
facebook.com/QuietTimeRhymes
john@QuietTimeRhymes.com

www.ingramcontent.com/pod-product-compliance
Lightning Source LLC
Chambersburg PA
CBHW060043040426
42331CB00032B/2262